LEVEL 2 SCIENCE

LET'S READ AND FIND OUT

DROUGHTS

BY MELISSA STEWART · ILLUSTRATED BY ANDRÉ CEOLIN

HARPER

An Imprint of HarperCollinsPublishers

Special thanks to Kelly Helm Smith and Tonya Bernadt of the National Drought Mitigation Center in Lincoln, Nebraska, for their valuable assistance.

The Let's-Read-and-Find-Out Science book series was originated by Dr. Franklyn M. Branley, Astronomer Emeritus and former Chairman of the American Museum of Natural History–Hayden Planetarium, and was formerly co-edited by him and Dr. Roma Gans, Professor Emeritus of Childhood Education, Teachers College, Columbia University. Text and illustrations for each of the books in the series are checked for accuracy by an expert in the relevant field. For more information about Let's-Read-and-Find-Out Science books, write to HarperCollins Children's Books, 195 Broadway, New York, NY 10007, or visit our website at www.letsreadandfindout.com.

Let's Read-and-Find-Out Science® is a trademark of HarperCollins Publishers.

The artist used Adobe Photoshop to create the digital illustrations for this book.
Typography by Erica De Chavez
17 18 19 20 21 SCP 10 9 8 7 6 5 4 3 2 1 ❖ First Edition

For Tamar Mays, whose wisdom and patience
has enriched so many manuscripts—M.S.

For my wife, Gracy, and my son, Gabriel, who always stood by me.
For Mela, who helped me a lot on my career. For all the young
readers who are getting ready for the future.—A.C.

When will it rain? That was the question on everyone's mind. It had been weeks and weeks since the last real storm.

A couple of times a few scattered raindrops fell from the sky. But not enough. The water didn't even soak into the ground. There was a **drought**.

What is a drought? It's a long period of time with less rain or snow than usual. Most droughts last a few weeks or months, but some go on for years and years.

When a drought happens, the water level in lakes and rivers drops. The soil dries out. Plants wither and wilt. Animals have trouble finding water to drink.

No Snow = Drought?

Yep, it's true. In some parts of the world, melted snow is the main source of freshwater. If less snow than usual falls during the winter, plants and animals may struggle the next summer.

Droughts are most common in places that normally have hot, dry weather.

But they can happen in wetlands and rainforests too. That might sound strange, but remember, a drought means getting less rain than usual for a long time. That can happen anywhere!

When you look at Earth from space, the first color you notice is blue. That's because water covers almost three-quarters of our planet's surface.

There is water in the sky too. Earth's water is always on the go. It moves from the ocean to the air to the land and then back again. This process is called the **water cycle**.

As the sun heats air above oceans, lakes, and rivers, liquid water **evaporates**. It changes into a gas called **water vapor**. Then it rises into the sky.

As the warm, moist air moves up, it starts to cool. Cool air can't hold as much moisture as warm air, so the water vapor **condenses**. It changes into tiny water droplets. The water droplets clump together and form clouds.

The drops grow bigger and bigger, heavier and heavier. Finally, they fall to the ground as rain.

Most of the world's water is in the oceans. So it's no surprise that most of the world's water vapor forms above warm ocean waters.

Winds push some of the moist air over land. When clouds form, rain falls on fields and forests, cities and towns.

But wind patterns can shift. The way water flows through oceans can change. Ocean temperatures can rise or fall. Any of these changes may cause less rain to fall in some places. That's when a drought happens.

Where Is the World's Water?

To find out, fill a 1-gallon milk jug with water and pretend it's all the water on Earth.

1. Pour $\frac{1}{2}$ cup of the water into a measuring cup. This is all the freshwater in the world. The rest is ocean water. Use a marker to write "Ocean Water" on the jug.

2. Pour $\frac{1}{3}$ cup of water from the measuring cup into a plastic cup. This water is frozen as ice and snow. Write "Frozen Water" on the plastic cup.

3. Pour half the water still in the measuring cup into a second plastic cup. This water is trapped in the soil or in the air as water vapor. Write "Trapped Water" on the second plastic cup.

4. The water left in the measuring cup is all the freshwater in the world's lakes, rivers, and underground sources. Now you know why we need to protect our drinking water!

A drought doesn't happen all at once. It builds up slowly over time.

At first, streams dry up and plants droop. If the rain returns at this point, people barely notice.

But the longer a drought lasts, the more trouble it causes. Heat bakes the soil until it cracks. Then plants begin to die. Their shriveled roots no longer hold soil in place.

Deadly Danger

When plants become brown and brittle, a lightning strike can spark a wildfire. The flames spread quickly through a forest of dry trees. They destroy everything in their path.

Wind picks up the dry, loose soil and blows it through the air. Sometimes a giant dust storm forms, causing the sky to go dark. Dirt and pebbles pelt people's bodies. The dust can bury roads and clog car engines.

COLORADO

KANSAS

TEXAS   OKLAHOMA

Did You Know?

In April 2014, a wall of dust and dirt whipped across five states. The giant dust storm blocked out the sun for hours. It knocked down trees and pummeled crops. Schools and businesses closed, but people couldn't get home. Traffic sat still on roads and highways.

When plants die, rabbits, squirrels, and other plant eaters have trouble finding food. Some may starve. After a while, foxes, hawks, and other predators start to die too. They can't live without food and water.

We depend on water too. We drink it every day. We also use it to clean our food, our clothes, our homes, and ourselves.

Farmers need water to grow crops. Companies use it to make products. During a drought, there may not be enough water to do all these things. That's why it's important to plan ahead.

In places where droughts are common, towns build dams to store water for times when it is needed. Homeowners plant trees and shrubs that don't need much water to grow. Farmers plant crops that will survive during hot, dry weather.

Did You Know?

You could live for a month without food. But you could die in less than a week if you didn't drink any water or eat any foods that contain water.

Scientists are always on the lookout for signs of drought. They use satellites in space to watch weather patterns all over the world.

Scientists also pay close attention to changes in the oceans.

Scientists measure how much rain falls. They check water levels in rivers and lakes. They keep track of moisture in the soil.

Scientists work hard to predict droughts before they start, giving people time to prepare.

You Can Measure Rainfall

1. Thoroughly clean a large plastic jar, such as a peanut butter jar.

2. Ask an adult to cut a large soda bottle in half. Turn the top half of the soda bottle upside down and place it inside the jar. The soda-bottle funnel will catch raindrops.

3. Use a ruler and a permanent marker to mark $\frac{1}{2}$-inch divisions along the side of the jar.

4. Place the jar in an open area outdoors. After the next rainstorm, check the jar to see how much rain fell.

During a drought, everyone tries to use less water. Families don't wash their cars or fill their swimming pools. They may stop watering their lawns. Shopkeepers sweep sidewalks instead of washing them. When everyone makes changes like these, there is more water for drinking and cooking.

We can't stop droughts from happening. They are a natural part of our world's weather. But we can plan ahead. If we use water wisely, droughts will cause fewer problems in the future.

Activities to Try

Cloud in a Jar

Believe it or not, you can make a cloud in your kitchen. Here's how:

1. Ask an adult to help you boil some water in a teakettle.

2. After the water has cooled just a bit, ask the adult to fill a measuring cup to the $\frac{1}{2}$-cup mark.

3. Carefully add the water to a large glass jar.

4. Place a metal pie pan on top of the jar, and add 10 to 12 ice cubes to the pan.

5. Wait two minutes and then shine a flashlight through the jar. What do you see?

A cloud forms in the sky when warm, moist air comes into contact with cool air. And that's exactly what happens in this activity.

How Much Water?

How much water could you save by turning off the water while you brush your teeth? To find out:

1. After blocking the drain in your bathroom sink, turn on the faucet and brush your teeth with the water running.

2. Use a measuring cup to scoop up water in the sink. After recording how much water is in the cup, pour the water into a bucket.

3. Repeat this process until the sink is empty. Then do some math to find out how much water you collected. (Hint: 16 cups = 1 gallon)

4. Now brush your teeth a second time. Turn off the water after wetting your toothbrush. Then turn it on to rinse your brush when you are done.

5. Use a measuring cup to scoop up water in the sink. After recording how much water is in the cup, pour the water into a bucket.

6. Repeat this process until the sink is empty. Then do some math to find out how much water you collected. Subtract this number from the number you calculated in step 3. That's the amount of water you could save every time you brush your teeth.

GLOSSARY

Condense—to change from a gas to a liquid

Evaporate—to change from a liquid to a gas

Drought—a long period of time with less rain or snow than usual

Water cycle—the constant movement of water between air, land, and sea

Water vapor—the gas form of water

FIND OUT MORE

Drought for Kids

http://drought.unl.edu/droughtforkids.aspx

Learn about the water cycle, what causes droughts, and how scientists study droughts.

HOW YOU CAN SAVE WATER

Turn off the water while you brush your teeth.

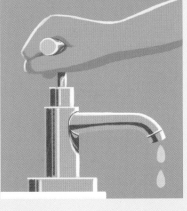

Take short showers instead of baths.

Wear clothes more than once before you wash them.

Don't run the dishwasher unless it's full.

Collect rainwater and use it to water plants.

Be sure to look for all of these books in the
Let's-Read-and-Find-Out Science series:

 The Human Body:
How Many Teeth?
I'm Growing!
My Feet
My Five Senses
My Hands
Sleep Is for Everyone
What's For Lunch?

Plants and Animals:
Animals in Winter
Baby Whales Drink Milk
Big Tracks, Little Tracks
Bugs Are Insects
Dinosaurs Big and Small
Ducks Don't Get Wet
Fireflies in the Night
From Caterpillar to Butterfly
From Seed to Pumpkin
From Tadpole to Frog
How Animal Babies Stay Safe
How a Seed Grows
A Nest Full of Eggs
Starfish
A Tree Is a Plant
What Lives in a Shell?
What's Alive?
What's It Like to Be a Fish?
Where Are the Night Animals?
Where Do Chicks Come From?

The World Around Us:
Air Is All Around You
The Big Dipper
Clouds
Is There Life in Outer Space?
Pop!
Snow Is Falling
Sounds All Around
The Sun and the Moon
What Makes a Shadow?

 The Human Body:
A Drop of Blood
Germs Make Me Sick!
Hear Your Heart
The Skeleton Inside You
What Happens to a Hamburger?
Why I Sneeze, Shiver, Hiccup, and Yawn
Your Skin and Mine

Plants and Animals:
Almost Gone
Ant Cities
Be a Friend to Trees
Chirping Crickets
Corn Is Maize
Dolphin Talk
Honey in a Hive
How Do Apples Grow?
How Do Birds Find Their Way?
Life in a Coral Reef
Look Out for Turtles!
Milk from Cow to Carton
An Octopus Is Amazing
Penguin Chick
Sharks Have Six Senses
Snakes Are Hunters
Spinning Spiders
Sponges Are Skeletons
What Color Is Camouflage?
Who Eats What?
Who Lives in an Alligator Hole?
Why Do Leaves Change Color?
Why Frogs Are Wet
Wiggling Worms at Work
Zipping, Zapping, Zooming Bats

Dinosaurs:
Did Dinosaurs Have Feathers?
Digging Up Dinosaurs
Dinosaur Bones
Dinosaur Tracks
Dinosaurs Are Different
Fossils Tell of Long Ago
My Visit to the Dinosaurs
What Happened to the Dinosaurs?
Where Did Dinosaurs Come From?

Space:
Floating in Space
The International Space Station
Mission to Mars
The Moon Seems to Change
The Planets in Our Solar System
The Sky Is Full of Stars
The Sun
What Makes Day and Night
What the Moon Is Like

Weather and the Seasons:
Down Comes the Rain
Feel the Wind
Flash, Crash, Rumble, and Roll
Hurricane Watch
Sunshine Makes the Seasons
Tornado Alert
What Will the Weather Be?

Our Earth:
Archaeologists Dig for Clues
Droughts
Earthquakes
Flood Warning
Follow the Water from Brook to Ocean
How Deep Is the Ocean?
How Mountains Are Made
In the Rainforest
Let's Go Rock Collecting
Oil Spill!
Volcanoes
What Happens to Our Trash?
What's So Bad About Gasoline?
Where Do Polar Bears Live?
Why Are the Ice Caps Melting?
You're Aboard Spaceship Earth

The World Around Us:
Day Light, Night Light
Energy Makes Things Happen
Forces Make Things Move
Gravity Is a Mystery
How People Learned to Fly
Light Is All Around Us
Phones Keep Us Connected
Simple Machines
Switch On, Switch Off
What Is the World Made Of?
What Makes a Magnet?
Where Does the Garbage Go?